BERKSHIRE
IN PHOTOGRAPHS

JIM HELLIER

AMBERLEY

First published 2020

Amberley Publishing
The Hill, Stroud
Gloucestershire, GL5 4EP

www.amberley-books.com

Copyright © Jim Hellier, 2020

The right of Jim Hellier to be identified as the Author of this work has been
asserted in accordance with the Copyrights, Designs and Patents Act 1988.

ISBN 978 1 4456 9430 6 (print)
ISBN 978 1 4456 9431 3 (ebook)

British Library Cataloguing in Publication Data.
A catalogue record for this book is available from the British Library.

Typesetting by Aura Technology and Software Services, India.
Printed in the UK.

ACKNOWLEDGEMENTS

I would like to thank the staff at Amberley Publishing and all my friends and family who helped me produce this book.

ABOUT THE AUTHOR

Jim took his first transparencies on a visit to Windsor Castle at the age of eleven with a Kodak Instamatic. This led to a lifelong passion for photography, although Jim did not go professional until later in life. After working as a building surveyor for one of the largest water companies in the UK, he took the opportunity to take an early retirement, which enabled him to take up photography full time.

He has always primarily been a landscape and travel photographer, though he has also worked with well-known fashion and fine art photographer Jerry Mason. These collaborations included travels to the Bahamas, Miami and the south of France – one of Jim's favourite locations.

Jim's landscape and travel work has been published in magazines such as *This England*, *Canal and Riverboat* and *French Life*. Some of the calendar companies that use Jim's images include Brunel Publishing, Rose of Colchester, Bemrose and Carousel Calendars.

Jim has also written e-book guides to photography and runs landscape photography courses.

INTRODUCTION

Within this book you will find many wonderful landscape images that I have captured with my camera while on my travels around the county of Berkshire. I have lived in this area for the last forty-plus years and I am still finding places of outstanding natural beauty that take my breath away. This is because Berkshire is an ancient county with sites that go back to Neolithic times. One such town is Thatcham, which is one of the oldest continuously inhabited areas in the United Kingdom.

Many towns were established along the banks of the River Thames, which was a major trading route for the county. The completion of the Kennet & Avon Canal in 1810 opened cargo travel between London and Bristol, bringing new life and business to the area. Then, with the arrival of the Great Western Railway, industry started to boom. Today you can see that the county is home to many companies within diverse sectors of industry.

Berkshire received the title of 'Royal County' from Elizabeth II in 1957 due to the presence of Windsor Castle. The royal family have been in residence there in some guise since it was built by William the Conqueror. The first recorded monarch to live there was Henry I – William's fourth son.

Scattered around the county you will find evidence of a rich history, from Windsor Castle to Donnington Castle – the latter now in ruins. There are burial mounds known as long barrows that can still be found on the Berkshire Downs, and just on the county border you will find the small village of Silchester, which was once a Roman settlement, with its city walls and amphitheatre still visible today.

As a photographer I have found that living in such a county fuels my passion for landscape photography. Quite often I will find myself returning to places to capture multiple angles and different lighting to make sure that the beauty I see before my eyes is truly translated to the printed form. In this book I hope to show you many of the wonderful and unique features that have inspired me over the years, and caused me to travel the length and breadth of Berkshire, capturing famous sites such as Windsor Castle, Eton College – where the princes William and Harry attended school – and, of course, the magnificent River Thames.

In recent times Greenham Common has once again become a site of interest with the filming of the latest Star Wars films taking place there, adding to its already rich history and proving that it really is all about location, location, location.

I hope that you enjoy this compilation of some of my favourite landscape photographs of Berkshire with its diversity of urban and country areas, beautiful down lands, and sparkling rivers.

Bluebells, Aldworth

St Mary's, Aldworth

The old well, Aldworth

Wheat fields, Berkshire Downs

Aldermaston Lock, Kennet & Avon Canal

Kennet & Avon Canal, Aldermaston

Ashampstead Common

Bluebells, Ashampstead Common

Berkshire Downs at dawn

Bisham Sailing School

Bisham Abbey

All Saints, Bisham

Cottages by the River Pang, Bradfield

Poppies on the Berkshire Downs, Compton

Christchurch Bridge, Caversham

Reading Bridge at dusk

Reading Bridge

Cookham Lock

The Thames above Cookham Lock

Piper's Island

View from Combe Hill

Thatched cottage by the River Lambourn, East Garston

River Lambourn, East Garston

Windsor Town Bridge, Eton

Caversham swans

View from Walbury Hill, Combe

Walbury Hill

Donnington Castle

River Lambourn, Eastbury

Cottage by the River Lambourn, East Garston

Hurley Lock, River Thames

The Holies, Streatley

Footbridge over the River
Lambourn, Eastbury

Approach to Hurley Lock

Lambourn Valley

Caversham Bridge

Georgian Hungerford

Footbridge over the Kennet & Avon Canal, Hungerford

Timber-framed houses, Hungerford

Garston Turf Lock

Bridge and ford on the River Lambourn

Hurley & Temple Weir

Bridge 84, Kennet & Avon Canal, Hungerford

The old mill at Kintbury

Hungerford Wharf

Kintbury Lock, Kennet & Avon Canal

Sheffield Swing Bridge

Fountain, Maidenhead

Lambourn Downs

Waiting at Boulters Lock

Maidenhead Bridge

Kennet & Avon Canal, Sulhamstead

Lock Stock & Barrel, Newbury

Guards Eyot, Maidenhead

West Mills, Newbury

Old Granary, Newbury

Newbury Lock

Winter sunrise, Purley on Thames

Sunrise through the willows

The Queen's Swan Keepers at Mapledurham

Swan Keepers leaving Mapledurham Lock

West Mills, Newbury

Footbridge to Newbury Lock

River Pang at Pangbourne

River Pang meets the Thames

The Ridgeway on Berkshire Downs

Ridgeway sign at Streatley

OVERTON HILL
65KM 41MILES

IVINGHOE
BEACON
71KM 44MILES

BURY DOWN
10KM 6·2MILES

STREATLEY
3KM 1·9MILES

View from Walbury Hill

View from Combe Hill

West Mills, Newbury

Newbury Lock

African Queen, Mapledurham Lock

Bridge in Bridge Street, Newbury

Reading Abbey

Dawn at Pangbourne Meadows

Windsor Bridge

Salisbury Tower, Windsor Castle

Nunhide Farm, Sulham

The Pang passes through Pangbourne

Thames moorings, Pangbourne

Ridgeway on the Downs above Compton

Huntley & Palmers building, Reading

County Lock, Reading

Streatley Warren

River Kennet meets the Thames at Reading

Sixteenth-century cottages, Pangbourne

Narrowboat passing
through Reading

Footbridge over the Kennet & Avon Canal

Barge, Blakes Lock, Reading

Kennet & Avon Canal at Sulhamstead

Dawn over the Thames Valley

Thatched cottages, Streatley

St Denys, Stanford Dingley

Spring on the Thames Path

The Ridgeway at Streatley Warren

The Lion of Reading

Windsor Castle from the Brocas, Eton

Streatley Weir

The Bull at Streatley

Yattendon

The Swan Hotel, Streatley

Ridgeway at Streatley

Kennet & Avon Canal, near Tyle Mill

Misty dawn

The Warren, Streatley

Burghfield Sailing Club lake

Long walk to the Copper Horse

Sheffield Bottom Lock

Poppies, Thurle Down

Fishpond, Forbury Gardens

Wilder's Folly

Forbury Gardens

Kennet Spur to Blakes Quay

Thurle Down

Sonning Bridge, Berkshire–Oxfordshire border

Windsor Bridge

Windsor Castle from Home Park

Old well house, Yattendon

Royal Oak, Yattendon

Windsor town

Curfew Tower, Windsor Castle

The long walk, Windsor Great Park